D1523427

ASKING QUESTIONS ABOUT MEDIA

# ASKING QUESTIONS ABOUT BODY IMAGE IN ADVERTISING

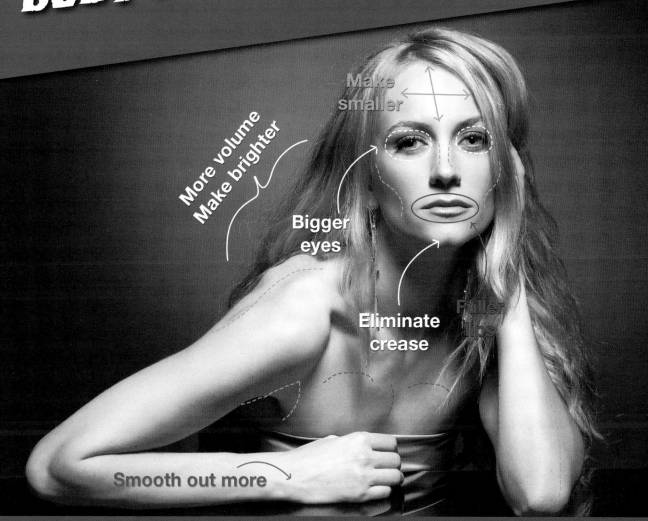

REBECCA RISSMAN

Published in the United States of America by Cherry Lake Publishing
Ann Arbor, Michigan
www.cherrylakepublishing.com

Consultants: Barb Palser, Digital Media Executive; Marla Conn, ReadAbility, Inc.
Editorial direction and book production: Red Line Editorial
Book design: Sleeping Bear Press

Photo Credits: Tatiana Gladskikh/Thinkstock, cover, 1; Michael Svoboda/iStockphoto, 5; Shutterstock Images, 6, 19;
Dove/PA Wire URN:8069588/AP Images, 8; Andrey Krav/iStockphoto, 11; iStockphoto, 12; Dmytro Zinkevych/
Shutterstock Images, 15; Mert Alas, Marcus Piggott/Rex Features/AP Images, 16; Christopher Futcher/iStockphoto, 20,
25; Helga Esteb/Shutterstock Images, 22; Iulian Valentin/Shutterstock Images, 26; Radu Bercan/Shutterstock Images, 28

Library of Congress Cataloging-in-Publication Data

Rissman, Rebecca.
  Asking questions about body image in advertising / by Rebecca Rissman.
      pages cm. -- (Asking questions about media)
  Audience: Grade 4 to 6.
  Includes bibliographical references and index.
  ISBN 978-1-63362-486-3 (hardcover : alk. paper) -- ISBN 978-1-63362-502-0 (pbk. : alk. paper) -- ISBN 978-1-63362-518-1
(pdf ebook) -- ISBN 978-1-63362-534-1 (hosted ebook)
  1.  Advertising--Juvenile literature. 2.  Advertising--Psychological aspects--Juvenile literature. 3.  Body image in
children--Juvenile literature.  I. Title.

  HF5822.R497 2015
  659.1--dc23

                              2015008363

Cherry Lake Publishing would like to acknowledge the work of
the Partnership for 21st Century Skills. Please visit www.p21.org
for more information.

Printed in the United States of America
Corporate Graphics

## ABOUT THE AUTHOR

Rebecca Rissman is an award-winning children's author and editor. She has written more than
200 books about history, culture, science, and art. Her book *Shapes in Sports* earned a starred
review from *Booklist*, and her series *Animal Spikes and Spines* received *Learning Magazine*'s 2013
Teachers' Choice Award for Children's Books. She lives in Portland, Oregon, with her husband and
daughter, and enjoys hiking, yoga, and cooking.

# TABLE OF CONTENTS

# CHAPTER 1

# BODY OF INFLUENCE

In 2012, Samsung Electronics released an amazing advertisement. It showed elite athletes training hard. Many ads use famous athletes to get your attention. But this one used participants in the 2012 Paralympic Games. Each of the athletes had overcome physical disabilities to become elite athletes. Uplifting music and dramatic footage contributed to the inspirational feeling of the ad. A tagline summarized its message: "Sport doesn't care who you are . . . Everyone can take part." The intent was to make viewers feel like they could be

*Advertisements can use different types of bodies to inspire different emotions.*

great, too. Samsung's commercial used an effective tool to inspire its viewers: body image.

Body image is the way a person thinks about his or her physical appearance. Religion, culture, weight, age, and gender identity can all affect a person's body image. The way that people feel about their bodies can influence the way they behave, the things they purchase, and what they believe about themselves and others.

One of the biggest influences on body image is the media. Television, the Internet, magazines, and newspapers are all different types of media.

*Magazines are one form of media that relies heavily on advertising.*

Advertisements are found in almost all media. They are created in order to sell a product or persuade a person to behave in a specific way. Ads can promote products such as clothing or food. They can also be used to sell experiences, such as vacations or concerts. Ads are used to persuade people to vote for politicians. And they are used to persuade people to change their behavior, such as to stop smoking or recycle.

## How Do You Feel?

Advertisements use different techniques to influence how you feel about yourself and their products. Emphasizing or **manipulating** body image is one of those techniques. Some ads use body image to make people feel insecure. Others use body image to inspire people to feel proud, or want to act. Some ads use body image to generate a sense of belonging to a larger group of people. And other ads use body image to make people feel alone. Advertisers do all of this as a way to sell their products.

*Dove used a diverse group of models to show how beauty standards can differ.*

How can you learn to see through the messages about body image in advertising? When you see an ad, ask yourself the following questions:

- Who created it, and why?
- What techniques did they use to get your attention?

- Who is represented in the ad, and who is left out?
- How might other people view this ad differently?

It's important to think critically about what you see. It will help you better understand these ads and what they hope to accomplish.

## DOVE'S CAMPAIGN FOR REAL BEAUTY

After a study showed that only 2 percent of women around the globe felt beautiful, the creators of Dove beauty products decided to act. Dove has worked hard to challenge the traditional beauty standards often found in advertising. Beauty standards are the typical physical features thought of as appealing. Today, Dove runs television, print, and digital ads featuring women of all shapes, ages, races, and sizes. The ads help sell Dove products. But they also help all women feel included in the conversation about beauty standards.

# CHAPTER 2

# BIG BUSINESS

Most of us are bombarded with advertisements all day long. Many of these ads use body image to sell a product. This technique is so common, it can be easy to overlook. But all ads are carefully created by businesses for specific purposes.

All advertisements have the same ultimate goal: to benefit the business or organization paying for them. Advertisers often create ads that use the human body to make viewers feel different emotions. Advertisers do this to persuade **consumers** to do what the advertisers want them to do. For example, a gorgeous model in a perfume ad might make a viewer feel insecure about how she looks. The viewer might respond by wanting to make herself more attractive to others. The advertisers hope she will purchase their perfume to help achieve that goal.

*It's almost impossible to escape advertising in today's world.*

*Retail giant Target was accused of being insensitive toward its plus-sized customers based on the names of colors it used to describe clothing.*

Making ads is big business. In fact, a 2012 survey found that more than 30 companies had annual advertising budgets of at least $1 billion. Many of these companies, such as department stores Macy's, JCPenney, and Sears, use body image in their ads to persuade consumers to buy their products.

## Case Study
# TARGET'S PLUS-SIZED MAKEOVER

Retailer Target faced harsh criticism in 2013. Some customers felt that the company portrayed **plus-sized** women in a negative light. One scandal involved labeling. Target sold a dress that was called "dark heather gray" in standard sizes. The same dress was called "manatee gray" in the plus sizes. Consumers were insulted by the comparison to the large sea mammal.

A plus-sized fashion blogger named Chastity Garner decided to act. She encouraged her readers to **boycott** Target. She felt that Target's negative portrayal of plus-sized bodies was harming the way women thought about themselves. Soon her message was being heard around the globe. Target responded by working with Garner and two other popular fashion bloggers. Together they created a stylish, affordable, and **empowering** line of plus-sized clothing. They advertised this new line with beautiful photos that featured the plus-sized bloggers modeling the clothing.

# CHAPTER 3

# GETTING YOUR ATTENTION

Every part of an advertisement is carefully chosen. Advertisers work with many elements in every commercial, billboard, and online ad. They use color, music, movement, lighting, words, camera angle, and bodies to get your attention.

Many advertisements use the human body to get people to pay attention. Some emphasize the models' attractiveness. These ads use alluring bodies to make you interested. Then they show you the product that they want you to buy. Ads for products ranging from

*Advertisers use many different elements to get your attention with an ad.*

cologne to toothpaste can use this type of appeal to sell their products.

But ads don't just use bodies for their attractiveness. They also use them to inspire. In 2015, Microsoft debuted a television ad showing a young boy growing up with **prosthetic** legs. The high-tech legs were designed by Microsoft. This ad also featured inspiring music, smart dialogue, and a cute, smiling star. The human body featured in this ad was used to draw the viewer's focus. It was also used to make them feel good about the

boy's amazing accomplishments and—by extension—
Microsoft, which made those accomplishments possible.

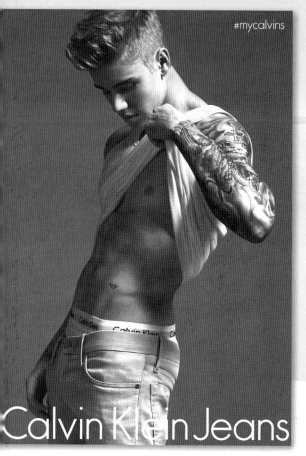

*This ad caused a controversy over whether the image of Justin Bieber's body had been manipulated.*

Body image can be used in ads to get a consumer's attention in many different ways. Viewers can be shocked, impressed, scared, or made to feel insecure by bodies in ads. In order to become a savvy consumer, you need to learn to see through these techniques.

The next time you see an ad, think about the first thing you noticed. If it had to do with body image, did it make you feel good or bad about yourself? Did you identify with the body in the ad? Did you feel as though you were being compared to it? Was the comparison favorable or unfavorable? Did the colors, music, movement, and words in the ad make you feel energized and excited? Sad or insecure? And what would the advertiser have to gain by generating those feelings in you? Learning to think about how the elements in ads make you feel is a great way to think critically about them and what they're selling.

## JUSTIN BIEBER'S CALVIN KLEIN AD SCANDAL

In 2014, pop star Justin Bieber appeared in advertisements for Calvin Klein jeans and underwear. His muscular, almost nude body caught the viewer's attention. He told his fans that he prepared for the modeling job by working out. However, soon after the ad appeared, someone claiming to own the original images from that photo shoot leaked them to the media. It looked as if the images had been altered to make Bieber appear more muscular. Bieber then said the leaked photos were fake. Regardless of which is true, it shows that body image is an important issue for both men and women.

# CHAPTER 4

# RECOGNIZING PERSPECTIVE

When you see a cosmetics ad, you might simply observe that it is selling makeup. However, what would you notice if you took a closer look? You might see that the ad uses body image to represent a specific set of values, point of view, and lifestyle. This may affect how you see the ad, how it makes you feel, and whether you want to purchase what the ad is selling.

An example of this can be found in a Neutrogena ad. It features a close-up of actress Julie Bowen's face. She looks thin, calm, and healthy. The text next to her says,

"Makeup that actually improves your skin." One of the values implied in this ad is that a person's appearance is important. It also implies that if you aren't happy with your appearance, you should buy makeup to improve it.

*Julie Bowen is the star of an ad campaign for Neutrogena products.*

The point of view shown here is that of a thin, healthy, Caucasian woman. The lifestyle depicted is that of a person wealthy enough to purchase name-brand cosmetics.

Thinking about who is not represented in an ad is a good way to understand the **perspective** of the ad. People of color, men, the elderly, and people who are not

*Advertisers sometimes are challenged to appeal to diverse groups of people, but more often ads are targeted to a specific type of consumer.*

## RACE IN ADVERTISING

In the past, most advertising featured Caucasian actors and models. Today, many ads feature people of different races. This is partly because viewers want to see more diversity. But it is also for business reasons. Advertisers know that actors and models who appeal to the viewer will attract new customers. Still, advertising has a long way to go until it is fully representative of the population.

wealthy are among the groups left out of the Neutrogena ad. The advertisers behind this message did not try to appeal to these audiences in their ad. They wanted an ad that would identify with the lifestyle, values, and point of view of a different type of consumer—one who is more likely to purchase Neutrogena products.

Ads that show models who are not traditionally beautiful, or who are elderly, disabled, overweight, or from an ethnic minority are often surprising to viewers. These advertisements catch the viewer's attention, but not because they are good at selling a product. They catch viewers off guard because they are different.

*Actress Lauren Hutton was an unconventional choice to model Lucky Brand jeans in 2013.*

Some advertisers have begun using this to their advantage. For example, when Lucky Brand featured 69-year-old actress Lauren Hutton in a 2013 ad, the company made headlines. Although people talked about Lucky's unique choice of model rather than the clothes she was selling, it still got people talking about the brand.

How can you see through the ads to understand the meaning behind them? When bodies are portrayed in ads, try to notice the point of view, values, and lifestyles that are being featured in the ad. Do you think the advertisers want you to identify with the body you're looking at? Should you aim to look like the model? Or are they showing you this body to make you feel better about your own? Asking these questions can help you understand all of the messages contained within ads. And it might change the way you think about some products. For example, does your favorite cosmetics company use models that look like you? What does that tell you about whether its products are right for you?

## JENNIFER HUDSON'S WEIGHT WATCHERS ADS

When singer Jennifer Hudson signed on as spokesperson for Weight Watchers, she lost 80 pounds. Soon, she began to receive **endorsement** deals for other products. Looking back, she said, "I never thought I was overweight. I thought my old look was pretty normal. That was how all the girls looked growing up in Chicago." Companies had overlooked Hudson because of her size. Discrimination based on a person's weight is known as **sizeism**. Hudson's rise to fame highlighted how sizeism affected her career.

# Mixed Messages

Have you ever watched television in a public place, such as a restaurant or airport? If so, you might have observed that the people around you had different reactions to the commercials you saw. This is because every person has his or her own unique perspective on the world. Your background, religion, race, gender, and age all affect the way you see things. This is especially true when it comes to body image in advertising. The way a fitness model reacts to a swimsuit advertisement

*Different people will have different reactions to what they see in the media.*

might be very different from the way an elderly person responds.

Many ads feature positive messages about body image. These often encourage viewers to identify with the bodies shown in the ads, whether the models appear to be picture-perfect or flawed. Other empowering ads feature a diverse range of bodies that make the viewer feel as though his or her unique perspective is being included. Ads that use body image for a positive effect can make consumers feel happy, comfortable, or

*Image enhancement software can remove a model's flaws and create an unrealistic standard of beauty.*

confident. These positive emotions can motivate people to spend money.

Other ads use body image in a way that negatively affects the viewer. Ads that show extremely thin, young, and flawless models create standards of beauty that are unrealistic. Many people who see these ads feel as though they can never look as beautiful or perfect as the models or celebrities being shown. The use of **Photoshop** and other image enhancement software make this problem even worse. This technology is used to remove visible flaws, such as acne and **cellulite**, and also often reshape models' bodies to make them appear thinner.

Ads that represent only one body type, race, age, or ability level can also make people feel negative about

## CASE STUDY
# BARBIE'S MAKEOVER

Barbie dolls have been popular children's toys since 1959. However, the doll has been criticized for contributing to negative body image among young girls. Barbie's curvy hips, large bust, and tiny waist are extremely exaggerated. Lately, Barbie's popularity has declined. This may be due to a new understanding of how body image affects young minds.

While Barbie's sales fell, other dolls that feature more realistic body types emerged. Lammily, also known as "Average Barbie," is a doll that has the proportions of the average 19-year-old woman's body. The doll comes with stickers for cellulite, tattoos, and acne. The makers of Lammily are hoping to spread the message that average is beautiful, too.

their own body image. People who are typically underrepresented in advertisements might feel as though the companies behind the ads do not care about their concerns.

*Barbie dolls have been criticized for creating distorted body images in young girls.*

When people feel negative about their body image, they may respond by purchasing products to improve their appearance or hide what they think are flaws. Advertisers know this. Ads for diet pills or exercise clothing often feature images that might make people feel bad about themselves, hoping to inspire them to purchase that product.

Advertisements can be funny, scary, sad, or heartwarming. They can be extremely entertaining and thought-provoking. For these reasons, they can be an enjoyable type of media. However, it is always important to recognize how they use body image to affect your opinion of yourself and of their brand. Always remember where the ads come from, who they are intended for, and what they are trying to accomplish.

# THINK ABOUT IT

When you see an ad that features attractive models, think about who made it. What do the creators have to gain from the ad? Could a different approach to the ad be just as effective?

Examine how the ad uses the models' bodies and attractiveness to get your attention. Does that have anything to do with the product being advertised?

Consider how an ad relies on body image to reach you. Does watching it make you want to look more like the models? Less like them? How do you think the ad's creators want to affect how you view your own body?

Think about how an ad might be interpreted by different types of people. Does that tell you more about who is being targeted? Do advertisers use body image to appeal to certain types of audiences more than others?

# LEARN MORE

## FURTHER READING

Gay, Kathlyn. *Body Image and Appearance.* Metuchen, NJ: Scarecrow Press, 2012.

Lankford, Ronnie D. *Body Image.* San Diego, CA: Lucent Books, 2010.

Palser, Barb. *Selling Ourselves: Marketing Body Images.* Mankato, MN: Compass Point, 2012.

## WEB LINKS

**Advertising and Disability**
www.advertisinganddisability.com/
This insightful blog examines how disability is portrayed in advertising.

**The Illusionists**
www.theillusionists.org/tag/photoshop/
Watch videos and read more about how the advertising industry alters images.

**Media Smarts: Talking to Kids about Media and Body Image—Tip Sheet**
www.mediasmarts.ca/teacher-resources/talking-kids-about-media-body-image-tip-sheet
This helpful tip sheet gives adults information on how to address body image issues with children.

# GLOSSARY

**boycott (BOI-kot)** to refuse to buy something or take part in something as a way of making a protest

**cellulite (SEL-yuh-lite)** fat that is close to the surface of the skin and that makes the skin slightly bumpy

**consumers (kuhn-SOO-murz)** people who buy and use products and services

**empowering (em-POU-ur-ing)** giving someone the feeling of power, strength, or ability

**endorsement (en-DORSS-muhnt)** support or approval, often from a celebrity for a company or product

**manipulating (muh-NIP-yuh-late-ing)** influencing something for a specific purpose

**perspective (pur-SPEK-tiv)** a particular way of looking at a situation

**Photoshop (FOH-toh-shop)** a computer program used to alter digital images

**plus-sized (PLUHSS-sized)** extra large, as in clothing or body shape

**prosthetic (pross-THET-ik)** artificial, as in a device used to replace a body part

**sizeism (SIZE-iz-uhm)** discrimination based on a person's size

# INDEX

[ 21ST CENTURY SKILLS LIBRARY ]